# KIM DUKE

# A Fine Mess

## AN ODD LITTLE BOOK ON
## SURVIVING LIFE'S DISASTERS

bhc
press

Livonia, Michigan

p. 47: London, England during the Blitz of WWII. Photo of woman drinking from a cup. Reprinted by permission of Royston Leonard/mediadrumimages. All rights reserved.

Edited by Darby O'Shaughnessy
Illustrated by Rosario Soley

## A FINE MESS
Copyright © 2020 Kim Duke

Published by BHC Press

Library of Congress Control Number:
2018948477

ISBN: 978-1-64397-097-4 (Hardcover)
ISBN: 978-1-947727-76-2 (Softcover)
ISBN: 978-1-948540-30-8 (Ebook)

For information, write:
BHC Press
885 Penniman #5505
Plymouth, MI 48170

Visit the publisher:
www.bhcpress.com

For Carol S. and Evelyn R.
*You made a difference.*

You're in
A Fine Mess!

You're reading this book, which means that some-way, somehow—you've had your world blown apart.

You're shocked, confused, enraged, embarrassed, guilty, insecure, depressed, ashamed, fearful, grief-stricken, humiliated. You're frozen, lost, sad or numb, alone, in a fog, in denial—
just to mention a few off the top of my head.

Acceptance sometimes dances briefly around the edges, but . . .

There are so many ways to experience disaster, aren't there?

What has set *you* back?
Crushed *you*?
Flattened *you* like a f*#%ing pancake?

Bankruptcy. Illness. House Burned Down. Death. Divorce. Fired. Loss of Limb. A Shitty Diagnosis. Flood. Volcano. Hurricane. Lightning. Tornado. Earthquake. Borrowed Money and Can't Ever Pay It Back. Loss of Libido. Loss of Reputation. Accident. Blew the Interview. He Read the Diary. Rags-to-riches-to-rags. Dumped by a Friend. Dumped by a Lover. The Tax People are After You. Fall from Grace. Failure. Failed to Show Up. Failed to Comprehend the Consequences. Heartbreak. Heartache. Vasectomy Didn't Work. Arrested. Arm Was Eaten by A Shark*. Thesis Bombed. Lost Your Business. Didn't Win the Lottery. The Bank Foreclosed on Your House. Grandma Left the Inheritance to Her Cat.

There are far too many disasters to list here.

*Remember the twelve-year-old surfer who lost her arm from a shark attack?

## Now that's A Fine Mess.

I can honestly say I've never been anyone's lunch.

Here's a space to add
your own Fine Mess:

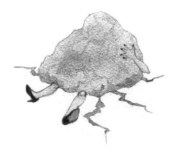

Don't fret if you think
your Fine Mess is too small . . .

. . . or too big.

A disaster is
whatever feels like a disaster to you.

Do you fantasize about *how* to make your great escape?

Plane, train, automobile, horse, tank, motorcycle, boat, submarine, blimp, bicycle, kite, hot-air balloon, skate, rocket, get-away car, helicopter, parachute, scuba dive, zip-line, swim, ski, swing like Tarzan, run away to the circus, magically disappear, hide, dig, fly?

My favorite escape fantasy was
wishing I could hop into a time-machine.

SOMEWHERE 06.06.1966

But as Robert Frost reminds us...

# The only way out

# IS THROUGH

ROBERT FROST

Fine Messes have the common thread
of being accidental journeys.

No one ever intends to end up in A Fine Mess.

No one wakes up in the morning, yawns, and says,
"Today looks like a *perfect* day
to get into A Fine Mess."

Fine Messes are conniving.

And they have dreadful manners.

They like to circle around and push your
face in the mud when you're not looking.

Things feel incredibly dark when
you're in the midst of a disaster.

Or when you're in its surreal,
alien aftermath.


But hope is waiting in the wings.

Barn BURNT DOWN, now I can see the Moon

TEXAN SAYING

On social media, an old friend recently posted
a picture of firetrucks in front of her apartment
building with this comment:

"I don't smoke anymore,
so I didn't start the fire,
this time."

Several years ago, she went out and acciden-
tally left a cigarette burning in her living room.
When she came home, her entire apartment had
burned to a crisp. She and several other tenants
were homeless for months, and her cat was
missing.

That was A Fine Mess indeed.

My biggest
disaster?

There have been a few Fine Messes in my life. But by far, the biggest and nastiest happened a few weeks after I visited the Tate Britain Museum in London, England.

I was at the museum with a client, and we were goofing around and laughing at a ridiculously huge ass sculpture that had just won a famous £100,000 prize ($130,000).

I actually stood directly underneath it.

Two weeks after I flew home to Canada, I received a breast cancer diagnosis, only a month after I turned fifty. Happy *f*#%ing* birthday.

I went from living my beautiful life to:

> *having both of my breasts removed;*
> *spending twenty days a month*
> *for five months bald and sick in bed from chemotherapy; and then*
> *twenty days of having my chest wall blasted with radiation.*

I practically lit up in the dark.

I was devastated, and so was everyone around me. My lovely aunt had also been diagnosed with cancer a few months earlier, so my family felt like we had stepped on a land mine.

I was trapped in hell, and some days I thought I would never find my way out.

But I did.

I am alive. Scarred, but alive.

> I don't look the same.
> I don't feel the same.

Some days I think people should call me "Franken-Kim."

But I still love life so very, very much.

No, I am not the same person I was before. Why?

Because every time a profound event happens in your life, that experience carves you.

And the deeper the experience—the deeper the carving.

You and I should both be on
Mount Rushmore by now.

I have no idea what
you're going through.

# BUT iT PROBABLY FEELS LiKE HELL.

You're probably asking this
two-word question to the Universe:

# WHY me?

Because you've lost something.

You've lost someone.

You've lost who you used to be.

# Fine Messes come in many nasty forms.

Many years ago, my dear friend Evelyn called and left a message for me, and I had been "too busy" to phone her.

I said to myself, "I'll call Ev back on the weekend."

*The weekend never came.*

*She killed herself on Wednesday.*

The crushing monster of guilt crawled on my back.

To come to a place of acceptance, to release the guilt I secretly carried took a long time.

Years.

Finally, realization dawned.

Did I love Ev? YES. Did I respect her? YES. Then I had to accept her choice—even though I didn't understand

Especially since I didn't understand.

My friend Phyllis said to me,

"Some years are for living in the question. Other years are for living in the answer."

I had to decide to live in the question of why Ev committed suicide.

I was never going to *understand* why.

I just had to accept the mystery of her decision.

Is there something mysterious hanging onto your back from your Fine Mess?

Do you secretly feel you invited
A Fine Mess into your life?
I remember telling a wonderful friend
who had written an insightful book
about her terrible childhood:

"I'd love to write a book to help
people, but I don't have a terrible
trauma story like you."

I wish I had never said *that* to the
Universe. What a dumb ass.

My comment was a hotline, Bat-phone
call to God, Who said,

"Well, Kim, I can sure fix that problem for you."

Me and my big mouth.

Or maybe you saw signs, but you
continued to ignore them.
Too busy?
Too scared?
Too delusional?
Too full of pride?


Or maybe—you played a
well-intentioned role that ended up
being the mistake of all mistakes?
And the result was a gigantic flop?
A failure so big it could land you in
the Sweden Museum of Failure?

Yes. There is such a place.

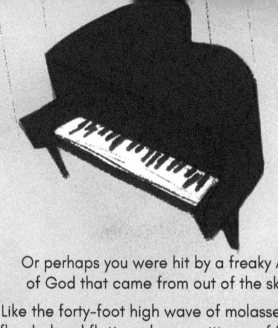

Or perhaps you were hit by a freaky Act of God that came from out of the sky?

Like the forty-foot high wave of molasses that flooded and flattened many citizens of Boston in 1919? That was a nasty and weird Fine Mess.

I feel like this happened to me, too.

You're not alone.
You're really not.
Suffering is a card
we all get dealt during
the poker game of life.

Sometimes rarely.
Sometimes often.
*But no one escapes.*

Take comfort in this dark and awkward truth—
and have compassion for those who
haven't had the disaster card dealt to
them *yet*. They are unprepared.

Realizing that they are inexperienced may
help you to not rip their heads off when
they spout trite, insensitive comments like:

*"What doesn't kill you,
makes you stronger."*

Visualizing these people
spontaneously bursting
into flames helps me.

# Falling flat isn't pretty.

Did you recently do a face plant like actress Jennifer Lawrence when she tripped on the stairs in her flowing pink evening gown to accept her Best Actress Oscar? Hopefully she'll laugh and shake her head at the memory when she's eighty.

Martha Stewart could tell you a few things about falling flat. Unexpected jail time will do that to a woman.

Falling flat on your face is painful.

But you can't stay there.

You'll get rained on.

Snowed on.

Used as a doormat.

Leaves will fall on you.

It's hell on your hair.

Yeah. It's time for you to get up.

"Fall 7 times,
get up 8."

JAPANESE PROVERB

*Fine Messes* happen to everyone:

Male and female.

Young and old.

Rich and poor.

Smart and not-so-smart.

People are affected by Fine Messes everyday, in every country of the world.

Hell, even birds fly into airplane engines. Fine Messes are attracted to us all.

# DON'T LET YOUR FINE MESS TAKE OVER.

I know a shark ate your arm.
Or the government cleaned you out.
Or your deadbeat fiancé
left you standing at the altar
wearing a dress worth
more than your car.

But you don't need to set up
house in your Fine Mess.
It happened *to* you,
but—it *isn't* you.

You don't have to become
a hermit in your misery.

Hermits hoard a lot of
newspapers. Also, they
start to smell funny.

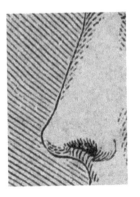

# You Can't Just Talk to the Walls.

Most Fine Messes feel private and inexplicable. You are shattered and talking to others can be difficult when you're splattered all over the floor. But talking to your dog, writing in your journal, calling 1-800-Madame-Zelda and conversing with the walls of your house can only take you so far.

You need to talk to someone who will listen and not judge you or try to fix you.

Be careful whom you choose. Many of your friends and family, or even your spouse—won't be able to handle it.

You probably already know the one person to whom you can reach out. If not—get yourself to a counselor.

You don't need to suffer twice. Enough of that.

You also don't need to go to the other extreme and talk about your Fine Mess to everyone who crosses your path.

When I received my cancer diagnosis, I secretly wanted to shout at everyone:

"How dare you bang my cart in the soup aisle! I just had my breasts cut off—you *Mother F\*#%er !!!*"

Or when people complained about their job, their boyfriend, their hair, how their vehicle wasn't running right—ordinary stuff that ordinary people talk about—*I felt like I was having an out-of-body experience and floating above them.*

I felt like I was from another planet.

Everything they talked about seemed so insignificant. I was dealing with giant life or death issues, and they were worried that their car insurance had gone up.

For the most part, this really pissed me off. Why? Because secretly, I wanted to go back to being like them.

But that is never, ever going to happen.

Finally, I calmed my rage-filled thoughts and remembered I wasn't the center of everyone's universe.

I had support. Loads of it.

*But this Fine Mess was really mine to figure out—*which meant I didn't have to discuss stuff when I didn't want to.

I didn't have to talk about my situation as much as before, and I didn't have to listen to other people's opinions.

*Because unless others had experienced the same thing—they really had no idea.*
And that was okay.

In fact, this insight made me realize that I needed to keep my mouth shut about other peoples' Fine Messes, too.

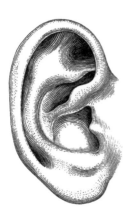

Why? Because one of the most important things we need when we're in a BIG, FAT FINE MESS is someone who is willing to *listen* vs. someone who talks about what we *should do* and *be*.

# You Are Not Choiceless.

For whatever reason, this Fine Mess is part of your life adventure.

You must find your way through it.
Whatever IT is—IT happened or is happening.

Now don't get grouchy. I know you don't want to think your Fine Mess is part of some fun adventure. But adventures aren't always fun.

Often, adventures are nasty and challenging and dangerous, and—they are full of choices. You have to choose to act.

Let's be honest.
Tight rope walking sucks.

YOU HAVE TO
DECIDE THAT
YOU AREN'T
GOING TO
SUFFER
THROUGH
THIS CRAP
FOR NOTHING.
YOU MUST FIND
SOME MEANING
AND PURPOSE
IN IT.

You may not know this, or perhaps
you haven't been told, but:

The world needs you.

Because of your Fine Mess, you've become
wise and strong in ways that others lack.

You have insight and resilience to share,
even if you're not ready to share it yet.

Somehow, you will find a way
to help yourself and others.
You will decide to transform—

—even if right now, you feel
bitter, bitter, bitter.

# Fine Messes are Cocoons of Opportunity.

Many people look at a pretty butterfly and smile, but they screw up their faces when they see a creepy, crawly caterpillar.

Baby, right now you're that caterpillar. You don't get to skip the steps of transformation.

## "POOF! I'm a butterfly."

Hell no.  The caterpillar has to go through some serious shit first.

It creates a cocoon and turns itself into...
Caterpillar Soup.

And from that gooey mess a
butterfly is created.

We're the same.

(Get a load of that.)

Chrysalis should really be called:

## Caterpillar Soup.

Disaster has forced you and me
into caterpillar soup.

We have to dissolve who we used to be.

We need to transform into something even more incredible.  But the process can be pretty disgusting and painful.  Somehow, I don't believe a caterpillar digesting itself is a walk in the park.

And—going into hiding appears to be a part of it.  So don't feel bad about secretly watching hours and hours of Netflix.

Time has a way of
changing things.

# Survival = Flexibility.

You may be asking yourself,

*"How will I survive this?"*

You are in a tornado of emotions.
It sucks so much.

And then—

Slowly. Weirdly. Finally.

You will decide to accept your
new reality and adapt to it.

Life is sneaky like that.

# This is a Maned Wolf.

He looks like a fox on stilts.

You have something in common with the Maned Wolf.

Our long-legged fellow had to adapt to get these lanky legs to see over the tall grasses of the African Savannah for hunting.

You have to adapt
to what your
new situation
requires of you.

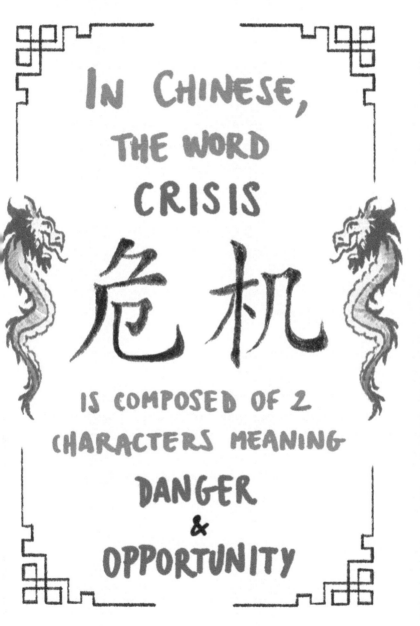

IN CHINESE, THE WORD CRISIS

危机

IS COMPOSED OF 2 CHARACTERS MEANING

DANGER & OPPORTUNITY

I was in a grocery store after I had just finished five months of chemo. I was pushing my cart and looking at ground hamburger, but my mind was swamped by thoughts of what had happened to me. I almost couldn't breathe.

I missed my beautiful, long, curly hair—for which I was famous— and I missed my boobs. I now had the chest of a ten-year-old boy. I felt mutilated. Watching everyone just go about their daily life while mine was such a pile of shit was so weird. My wig kept sliding around my head, and I could have burst into tears in the meat department.

And then a man walked past me, and something caught my eye.

I did not see his face; I saw him from behind.

He was missing his left arm. He had a prosthetic arm and a steel claw that pushed the grocery cart.

*He'd adapted. He wasn't crying by the broccoli.* I froze.

What were the odds of something like this happening?

I decided, in spite of it all, that I was lucky.

When you're put into the fire with disaster, either you are forged stronger or you melt.

How do I know? In my spare time, I weld.   My dad has been teaching me for several years.

Welding is the act of applying intense heat to transform and meld two metals together. Together they are forged stronger.

When you're going through your Fine Mess, *you* have to decide how *you* want to turn out.

Are you going to melt or meld?

*Somehow, making a decision changes the hardship.*

London, England during The Blitz of WWII

This woman was certainly in A Fine Mess.
I think her tea cup is giving her strength.

Strangely, books can save you.

Viktor Frankl is one of my mentors whose voice I keep hearing in my head. His thoughtful words helped me to survive the worst psychological and physical suffering of my life.

During World War II, the Nazis imprisoned young Jewish psychologist Viktor Frankl in concentration camps where he spent three years. During that time, he lost everyone he loved. Wife, parents, family and friends—all were murdered. And yet, Frankl felt a deep inner purpose. He decided to turn his ordeal and suffering into an observation of human behavior under extremely stressful circumstances.

He observed that some people who should have lived—didn't. And others, older, weaker, or ill—survived.

The difference?

*Those who found meaning in their experience tended to live.*

Everyone on this planet should read Frankl's book, *Man's Search for Meaning*, which he published a year after the war in 1946.

Thank you,
Viktor.

# Look for the Good.

One of my favorite authors is Heather Lende. In her book *Take Good Care of the Garden and the Dogs: A True Story of Bad Breaks and Small Miracles*, she writes about a life-threatening event that happened to her.

Lende almost died when a truck hit her as she was on her usual morning bike ride. Normal broke that day—as did her pelvis. The accident also happened on the day her first book was launched nationally in the USA. Without warning, joy and pain intersected.

She was flown to a Seattle, Washington hospital— 1000 miles from her home and family in Haines, Alaska. She then spent a year recovering in a nursing home of all places and in her own home.

I think we can safely say Lende had *A Fine Mess* on her hands.

But she chose to look for the good.

Will you?

A lovely friend of mine grew up in hardship that follows her around like a shadow. In the past few years: she lost her house; her husband had a malignant melanoma on his nose and required surgery; neither she nor her husband were able to work; their car broke down; she needed heart medication; they had to move to another city and live with friends; she had to give away her beloved cat.

She would call this A Fine Mess.

But something has happened in the midst of the chaos. The kindness of friends and family appeared.

She and her husband have not been alone during this trial.

They are loved. People are helping. All is not lost.

She told me recently on the phone, "I am such a lucky woman. I have Buddhism, my intellect, my books, my friends. I love my husband who is an amazing cook, and we both love the simple things in life. I am resilient, and I will get through this."

She will.

And so will you.

One summer when I was eighteen years old, I worked as a cleaner in a small local hospital.

Many of the patients were elderly, long-term, or terminally ill.

In one of the rooms was an older gentleman who was dying from stomach cancer. I'd been told by the nurses that he wasn't to eat anything because he was being fed intravenously. His stomach was gone, and he had a bag outside his paper-thin body.

I walked into his room one afternoon to mop the floor and saw him eating a Hershey chocolate bar. "Oh, no, Mr. Smith," I said. "You're not supposed to be eating that!"

He looked at me and put his finger in the air. He kept chewing. Then he reached under the covers and pulled out a container. He spat all the chewed-up chocolate into it and wiped his mouth. "It's okay. I may not be able to swallow the chocolate, but I can still taste it and then spit it out. I love chocolate." He grinned a big chocolatey smile at me.

I smiled back and left him to enjoy his chocolate. I didn't tell anyone.

A few years ago, I was in the Minneapolis Institute of Art and I saw several paintings of women with large pleated collars around their necks. A strange reminder that fashion for the most part, is absolutely stupid.

I wondered: Were they conforming, challenging, or adapting?

What you decide is really all about perspective. It's how you look at these women. They all most certainly would have found themselves in A Fine Mess at one point.

All I know is that I am super grateful that I don't have to get up every morning, drink my cup of coffee, and then put a gigantic, ruffled oil filter around my neck.

There's a lot of good in that.

# Step Outside Yourself.

When you're in A Fine Mess, it's mostly about you. Sometimes too much about you.

Not only do you drive yourself nuts, but you probably drive the people around you nuts, too. What's the fastest way to forget yourself and your troubles for a while?

*Go help someone else.*

Volunteer. Shovel someone's sidewalk. Buy some flowers and deliver them in person. Go read to children at a school. Take a senior to a movie. Rake some leaves for your neighbor. Bake a cake and give it away. Have people over for dinner. Compliment someone unexpectedly. Write a resume for someone who hates doing it.

Instead, step out and away from the craziness and into kindness.

Not only will you put a smile on someone else's face, but you'll probably put one on your own face, too.

I was twenty-six years old and sitting with my friend in an over-crowded coffee shop surrounded by books. The little spot was quirky with the comforting hum of conversation, the swoosh of the coffee steamers and the ring of the old-fashioned cash register. Little did I know a life-changing event was about to happen.

My friend Evelyn sat across from me warming her hands with her cup. She was patiently listening to me complain—yet again—about my narcissist live-in boyfriend. I was sad because I knew he didn't love me. He was extremely in love, though, with looking at himself in the mirror. I kept hoping he would wake up and say, "You're the best thing that's ever happened to me!" But both Evelyn and I knew he was never going to say that. I just had to get the guts to leave him. Evelyn gave me some wise advice. We laughed, and I felt some relief from the pressure on my chest because my lover didn't love me.

*I felt a tap on my shoulder.*

I looked behind and saw an elderly woman with her husband enjoying tea and cake.

Half of her face showed her keen intelligent eyes, her warm smile and the prettiness still residing in her seventy-something self. An earthquake had ravaged and collapsed the other half of her face, now a row of fallen buildings. Her left eyebrow, eyelid, cheek, mouth and chin sagged under the weight of a stroke.

She gave me a lop-sided smile and said slowly, "I'm sorry to interrupt, but I've been looking at your beautiful hair for an hour. I had to see if your face matched your hair, and it does. You're beautiful."

In that crowded, dishes-clanking coffee shop, I felt everything inside me go quiet. It was just she and I. My emotions went through their own sudden earthquake tremors. I felt grateful and selfish. Petty and thankful. Humbled and ridiculous. Overflowing with joy and sympathy, I cracked wide open.

With tears in my eyes, I clasped her hand and smiled.

"Thank you! I'm speechless. You're the beautiful one for saying this to me." We shared a few more words, and then I turned back to Ev. We just sat there, staring at each other.

"Can you believe what just happened?"

Evelyn smiled in her knowing way—and laughed.

"The Universe brings you what you need, Kim."

I wish I could say that I drove home and dumped my loser boyfriend that night. I didn't. I spent another ten months with him before we parted ways. But that kind, elderly woman was within me just the same. The words of a stranger with a paralysed face helped me to become unparalysed. The simple beauty of what she did that day has never left me.

She was kind to a stranger even though she was deep in her own Fine Mess.

*You need to help others, too.*

It gets you out of your tangled and obsessive thoughts.

(And after you've done your noble deeds—feel free to have a hot bath loaded with bubbles.)

# Nothing Really Is Ordinary.

An odd and wondrous thing happens after intense hardship: even if you thought you had been grateful before; even if you thought you appreciated the world around you.

After you've been to the bottom of whatever-it-is, and you rise, *everything looks different.*

*That you may find yourself attracted to the simplest things instead of the complicated—* doesn't mean you're less than.

Or that you're settling. Or giving up.

That you embrace the ordinary means that you're choosing to see what is really important.

You're here on this little blue marble, revolving around Earth's closest star at 67,000 miles per hour, in a galaxy surrounded by millions of other galaxies—and you have been blessed with the opportunity to be here.

Compared to the longevity of Earth, we have a life-span far less than that of a fruit fly's. We'd better make the most of it. Remember: We all are on this planet—all of us—we are all fruit flies, too. So there's really no sense in being envious of anyone or of not being grateful for our own fruit fly lives.

This Fine Mess
is part of your adventure—
as complicated as it may be.

A little reminder. You and I are here to live many beautiful and odd and sometimes sad experiences. Some we have no control over. But with so many, we do. *Look for the good in it all.*

We're here to hear children laugh, frogs croak. The ocean. Rain showers. Music of all kinds. To watch a bumblebee fly. See chickadees. Sunsets. Stars. Elephants. The smile on a dog's face. Sunrises. Storms. Santa. Candle light. Art. Cows. Dew drops. Christmas lights. Movies. Frost. Trees. Spider webs. The beauty of flowers. The shimmery midnight blue-black of a crow's feathers. To taste chocolate. Champagne. Eat cheese. Lemon pie. Enjoy ice-cream. Birthday cake. A bite of a homegrown tomato. Lemons. Crazy family dinners. A cold beer. The perfection of a hard-boiled egg. To fall off our bikes and skin our knees. Bake cookies with Grandma. Help others. Laugh till we cry. Travel. Lie in the grass on a warm summer's day. Share a smile. Read books. Sing. Lose someone we love. Skip a flat stone. Go fishing. Comfort someone. Make a friend. Lose a friend. Take long walks. Inhale the fragrance of autumn leaves. The smell of freshly mown grass. Fresh cut wood. Baking bread. Experience first love. Breakups. Broken hearts. Falling in love. Giving birth. Feeling snowflakes hit our tongues, the wind on our faces. Bubble baths. Warm, fuzzy sheets in the winter. The kiss on our cheek. Tears. A hug from mom. Being lifted into the air by dad. Sliding

into cool sheets in the summer. Soft skin. Soft
lips. A strong hand in ours.

Perfectly imperfect days that make up our lives—
and, this, whatever this Fine Mess is for you, is
part of it ALL.

# On, Crap.

Maybe your Fine Mess was a slow build, or maybe it happened in a flash. Either way—you've ended up in the same shitty spot.

You just want to send this shit-o-gram back.

Years ago, a psychic looked at my Tarot cards, and then she looked at my hands. She said,

> "You've had some hardship, but you will find your way. Even from manure piles, flowers shall bloom."

I am a farmer's daughter.
Which means I grew up smelling shit from cows, pigs, chickens and bison.

When I told my quietly gruff and loving father that I've always hated the smell of farm shit, he said,

"You should love the smell. It put you through college."

Har.

And then he said,

"You may not like it but shit has a job to do. It helps things grow."

"They tried to bury us.
They didn't know we were seeds."
— Mexican Proverb —

This Fine Mess
you're in?
Even. Shit. Has.
A. Job.

Here are some words to help you
through your Fine Mess:

Grit

Loveliness

Comfort

Backbone

Wonder

Perspective

Friendship

Guts

Relax

Patience

Gentleness

Whimsy

Courage

Creativity

Simplicity

Tenderness

Endurance

Gratitude

Laughter

Strength

Conquering

Beauty

Release

Inspiration

Fortitude

Curiosity

Acceptance

Bravery

Resilience

Healing

Determination

Gumption

Love

# Why Some People Frustrate You Right Now:

When you've experienced disaster, it's difficult to be around people who are caught in a web of self-importance—shocking but true.

Listening to them talk endlessly about their job, kids, bad haircut, the Christmas presents they didn't like or how someone cut them off in traffic makes your eyes glaze over at the best of times. But since your Fine Mess—your tolerance level is pretty much zero.

*Try not to judge.*
*You were there once.*

You can distance yourself from these people. If not physically, then at least mentally. You don't have to get caught up in their petty bragging and stresses. In fact, your Fine Mess is a big sign to release as much of it as you can.

For all you know, absorbing that stuff in the past may have been the roots of your disaster.

Instead, step back. Remind yourself of how you have overcome and/or how you will overcome your current shit show. You must keep the self-

absorbed people on the outer-limits of your life.
Give them a little kick into the next galaxy.
You've got bigger fish to fry. Your perspective
has changed.

Some people won't get it. You will lose some
friends. Maybe this has happened already:

- Your Fine Mess disrupts their lives.
- They are too uncomfortable with your Fine
  Mess.
- Or your Fine Mess reminds them that (gasp!)
  it could happen to their perfect life. Secretly
  they think you will hex them.

  *Note: The odds of them reading this book
     or buying it for you are slim-to-none.

So what can you do?  Let it go.

Try to be as kind as you can—but make sure you have filters to keep their crap out.

And just as people will leave your life (bye-bye!), others will become much closer to you—because they stepped into the fire with you when others stepped out.

Gratitude is a big part of A Fine Mess.  Probably you need to thank some people. Over and over.

They didn't abandon you.

They believe in you.

They help you through the hardship—which is why beautiful experiences *can* come out of Fine Messes.

*However, kind as you are, still feel free to make a little Ms. Mess doll of anyone really driving you nuts and poke pins in it.

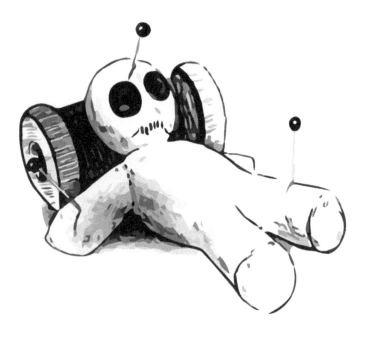

*It's OK. Just because you've experienced A Fine Mess doesn't mean you're Mother Teresa.

# Let Mother Nature Soften the Edges.

When you're in the middle of chaos, it is difficult to concentrate. Most of the time, you feel like your head is spinning. The stress is off the Richter scale. Everything feels jagged.

Instead of riding the endless roller coaster in your head, try this:

*Open the door and go outside.*

During the day—walk to a tree, flower, stone, pine cone, or whatever natural wonder crosses your path first. And then really look at it.

Immerse yourself in being an observer. See the poetry in a leaf, or in an ant marching by. (Resist the temptation to step on him!) And give yourself five minutes to just stand still and quietly watch the world around you.

And now look up. Way up.

Watch the clouds as if you were a child seeing them for the first time.

Notice how part of their beauty is the way they are constantly changing.

Later, when night has fallen, go outside again. Look up at the stars and spend five minutes in their company. Millions of stars are constantly shining - even when we forget about them during the day. Just as right now you are forgetting the finer points of yourself.

Simple wonders surround you in nature at every moment—even in the middle of your Fine Mess. Let them comfort you and show you how this, too, shall pass.

# The Beauty of Cracks.

I love the Japanese culture. They have the most lovely and unusual ways of looking at the ordinary.

They have a philosophy called *wabi-sabi*, which means to see the beauty within imperfection and impermanence.

They don't see decaying leaves, a scratched table, or an elderly woman with wrinkles as something ugly to be ignored or discarded.

I learned this from a wonderful friend.

Years ago, my friend Dennis shared some thoughtful Japanese phrases and philosophies. He is Japanese-Canadian and he has many creative passions. Dennis is a Renaissance Man as he is a musician, poet, writer, painter, potter and even folded paper turns into something beautiful in his hands. He sees everything as potential art material.

He said,

"We believe in *wabi-sabi*. That there is beauty in the flawed and imperfect."

I laughed and said, "So that's why we're friends!"

One year he made me a delicate and tiny pottery bowl and said, "If it ever breaks, just let me know and I'll *kintsugi* it."

Dennis explained *kintsugi* is a method of repairing a broken piece of pottery but instead of trying to hide the flaw–the break is accentuated with powdered gold and a special lacquer.

This is you. And definitely me.

Whether you were ready or not,
your cup has been emptied—
and it probably has a big crack in it.

My friend taught me that the word *mottainai* expresses regret when something is wasted and *mushin* means the acceptance of change.

Well, there you have it:

You're cracked. (*wabi-sabi*)

You don't want to waste your life
with regret. (*mottainai*)

You are open to repair your
cracks with gold. (*kintsugi*)

You're accepting of change—
even if you hate it. (*mushin*)

To feel cracked is perfectly okay.  You can join
me in the cracked-up club.   You'll find quite a
few of us.

I should call myself
Kintsugi Kim.

Now What ?

Are you on the other naked side of your Fine Mess?

You feel like Humpty Dumpty trying to put all your pieces back together again—except you can't find a glue that works.

And you certainly can't find all the fragments of your shattered self. You're pretty sure someone swept up a big piece and took it out to the trash. The people who love you and helped you through your Fine Mess seem to think it's all over and your life is back to normal.

You love them so much—you really do.

But you're still shell-shocked.

It's okay. You're not losing your mind.

You've experienced an accidental journey that parachuted you into a new country.

Old you. New you.

You don't get to carry much of the old you into your new country. You will have to release some people, beliefs, behaviors and other baggage. You're going to have to change your mind about what you used to take for granted.

Only the best of you is worth carrying. You have to leave the bulk of you behind. Some stuff you'll want to cling to but keep *only* what is essentially you. I'm bringing books, lipstick, and an attitude. You must move on and become a citizen of your new country. New friendships, new experiences and a new life await you.

But dual-citizenship isn't going to cut it here.

Give yourself time to figure out your Fine Mess.

Accidental journeys push us off course so that we have to figure out which course we want to be on. But don't let yourself get stuck looking behind you. (It hurts your neck. Or you may turn into a pillar of salt.)

You can rebuild. You can move forward. You can be proud of yourself. You can be the phoenix who rises gloriously from the ashes.

You can elevate and refine who you are and what you want. You can grow and learn from this shitty experience. Remember—even shit has a job.

A simple elegance and strength can come from your Fine Mess.

Wisdom, compassion and a greater understanding of the world tend to show up, too. You've got the battle scars to prove it.

You can choose to see your Fine Mess as a comma and not as a period.

The choice is yours.
And I think you're up for it.

Your Fine Mess?

Smoother seas
are ahead.

# Acknowledgments

How do you thank the people who saved you when you were thrown into the abyss? I could fill another book with all the kindnesses they did for me.

I would never have made it through my Fine Mess without the love and support of:

My husband, Rob, who is my anchor, and who told me I was beautiful even when I looked like a featherless, baby bird.

My parents Layne and Sylvia. Carol, Kelly, Carly, Megan, Merv and Tyler.

Marcia. Renee, Conor, Nora and Nolan. Robynn, Evan, Harper and Oliver. The Labossiere clan.

My incredible friends: Tina Pratt, Jo Dibblee, Martin & Ness Sawdon, Phyllis Knox, Andrea Varzari, Jo Paul, Debbie & Tommy Mrazek, Laurel & Frank Vespi, Michele McDougall, Jo-Ann Yewchuk, Grant & Val & Evan Simpson, Lynda & D'Arcy Kavanagh and many others who kept a steady stream of visits, physio, prayers, phone calls, house-cleaning, texts, videos, cards, books, flowers, food, packages in the mail, poetry, bad jokes, and Netflix suggestions rolling to me for over a year.

The specialists at the Alberta Cross Cancer Institute; surgeon Dr. Walter Yakimets, and nurse practitioner, Susan Horsman, for saving my life.

Writers whose words gave me hope and a laugh when I was at the edge of despair:  Maira Kalman, Anne Lamott, Sarah Ban Breathnach, Elizabeth Gilbert, Caitlin Moran, Heather Lende, Elizabeth Berg, Alexandra Stoddard and Flow magazine creators, Irene Smit and Astrid van der Hulst.

And my black knight
in shining fur,
Bentley, for
watching over
me all those long,
hard months.

# About the Author

Kim Duke is an international writer known for her easy and witty style when talking about tough stuff.

She's been covered by *Cosmopolitan*, NBC News, CTV, and CBC and her work has been featured on *The Globe and Mail* and the internet sensation, *Medium.com*.

She lives in Alberta, Canada with her husband and werewolf dog.

Find her online at her website:
thecomplicatedsimple.com

Lightning Source UK Ltd.
Milton Keynes UK
UKHW020652281020
372365UK00007B/227

9 781947 727762